P9-DOB-366

AN INDIAN WINTER

At Fort Clark in the heart of Indian country, Prince Maximilian, wearing a dark coat and hat, is introduced to a delegation of Hidatsa dignitaries. Karl Bodmer stands to his left. Behind them, with a mustache, is David Dreidoppel.

AN INDIAN WINTER

by Russell Freedman

Paintings and Drawings by Karl Bodmer

Holiday House / New York

For Tom Gullion
and Sybil

Printed in the United States of America
FIRST EDITION

Library of Congress Cataloging-in-Publication Data
Freedman, Russell.
An Indian Winter / Russell Freedman ; paintings and drawings by
Karl Bodmer.
p. cm.
Includes bibliographical references and index.
Summary: Relates the experiences of a German prince, his servant, and a young Swiss artist as they traveled through the Missouri River Valley in 1833 learning about the territory and its inhabitants and recording their impressions in words and pictures.
ISBN 0-8234-0930-9
1. Bodmer, Karl, 1809–1893—Journeys—Missouri River Valley—Juvenile literature. 2. Wied, Maximilian, Prinz von, 1782–1867—Journeys—Missouri River Valley—Juvenile literature. 3. Indians of North America—Missouri River Valley—Social life and customs—Juvenile literature 4. Missouri River Valley—Description and travel—Juvenile literature. 5. Travellers—Missouri River Valley—Biography—Juvenile literature. [1. Bodmer, Karl, 1809–1893—Journeys—Missouri River Valley. 2. Wied, Maximilian, Prinz von, 1782–1867—Journeys—Missouri River Valley. 3. Indians of North America—Missouri River Valley. 4. Missouri River Valley—Description and travel.] I. Bodmer, Karl, 1809–1893, ill.
II. Title.
E78.M82F74 1992 91-24205 CIP AC
917.804′2—dc20

JACKET ART: (front) *Mih-Tutta-Hang-Kusch*, Mandan Village;
(back) *Síh-Chidä, Mandan Man*

Contents

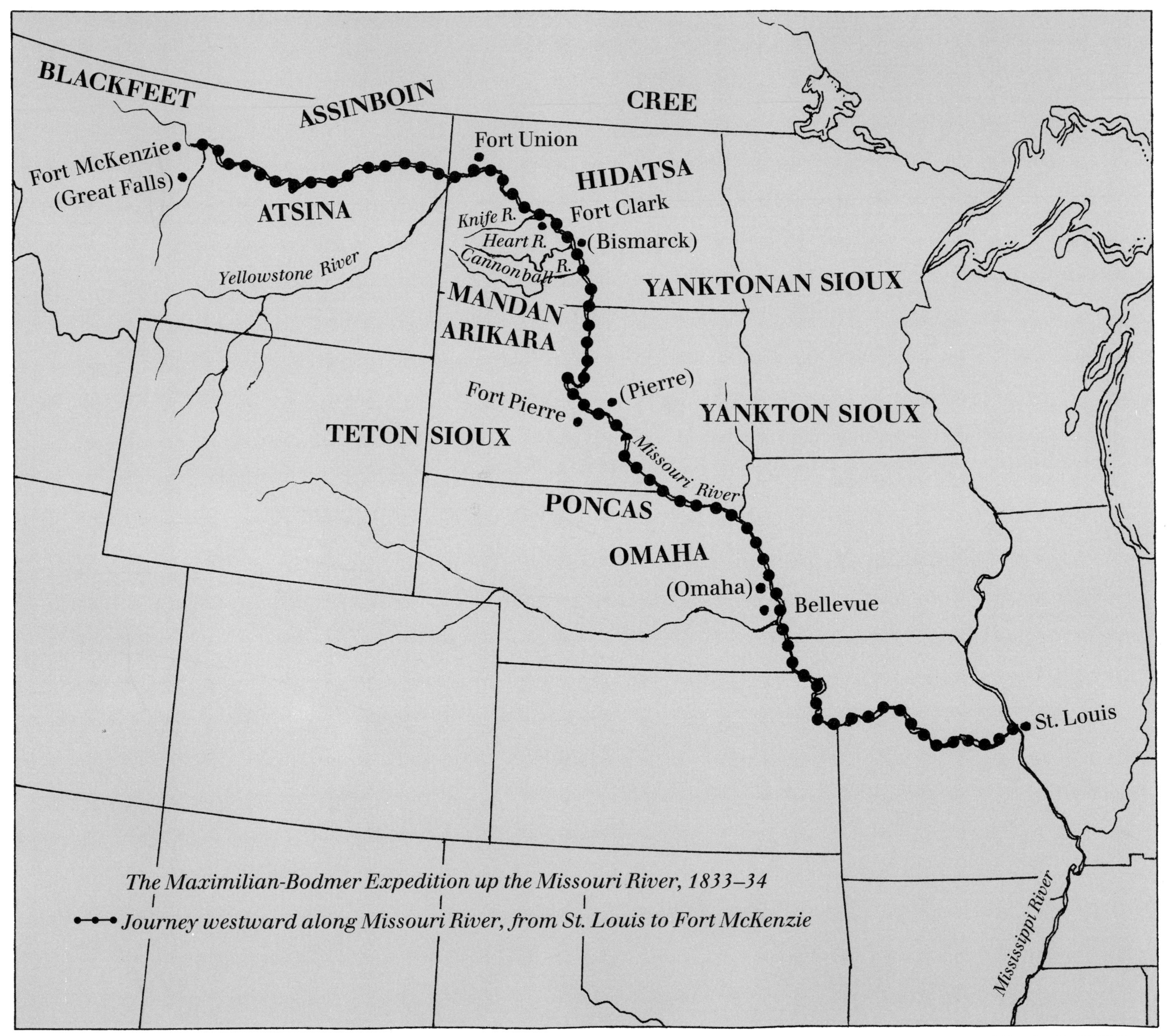

Map by Gail Gibbons

In 1833–34, Alexander Philipp Maximilian of Wied-Neuwied, a German prince, and Karl Bodmer, a Swiss artist, spent the winter with the Mandan Indians in what is today North Dakota. Maximilian kept a detailed journal. Bodmer painted portraits, landscapes, and scenes of everyday life. They viewed Native American life and culture through the eyes of European strangers, yet they were sympathetic observers who left a vivid word-and-picture record of their journey to the unspoiled western frontier. This is the story of their adventure and the people who befriended them.

All quotations, unless otherwise noted, are from Maximilian's published account of his North American expedition.

Russell Freedman
July 15, 1991

Sailing to America aboard the Janus, *Maximilian writes in his journal, using a barrel as a desk. The figure in the background appears to be Bodmer making a sketch.*

One
The Prince and the Painter

Maximilian, Prince of Wied, dreamed of meeting the Indians of North America. In his castle on the Rhine he would pore over maps and study travelers' reports as he planned his expedition to America's western frontier.

The prince was a highly educated man, a trained scientific observer, and a daring explorer. Since boyhood, he had pursued a lifelong passion for natural history and the study of native cultures.

In 1815, after fighting with the Prussian army in the Napoleonic Wars, Maximilian had sailed to South America. He spent two years exploring the tropical rain forests of Brazil, where he collected thousands of plant and animal specimens and shared campfire meals of roast monkey with the local Indians. Back home in Germany, he published a two-volume account of his Brazilian journey.

By 1832, he was ready to embark on the second great adventure of his life. This time he would visit the wilds of North America. He wanted to seek out those Plains Indians whom few whites had ever seen and record their tribal ways in words and pictures.

To illustrate the book he intended to write about his journey, Maximilian needed the services of a skilled artist. He hired Karl Bodmer, a promising young Swiss landscape painter. Bodmer had just turned twenty-three when he accepted the job. It offered him a chance to practice his craft while visiting a distant and little-known land. "He is a lively, very good man and companion, seems well educated, and is very pleasant and suitable for me," Maximilian wrote to his brother. "I am glad I picked him."

The third member of the party would be David Dreidoppel, Maximilian's loyal manservant. An expert hunter and taxidermist, he had accompanied the prince on his travels through Brazil.

The three men sailed from Holland to the New World in the spring of 1832 aboard the American ship *Janus*. They landed in Boston on the Fourth of July, in time to watch a noisy Independence Day celebration on Boston Common. From there they made their way across the United States by stagecoach, horseback, and riverboat. Bodmer began to sketch and paint scenes of American life. Maximilian collected natural history specimens and filled the pages of his journal with observations and descriptions. He celebrated his fiftieth birthday on September 23 while traveling through Pennsylvania. By then, he had accumulated five crates of specimens to ship back to Europe, including 170 birds, 43 turtles, 40 to 50 snakes, and about 40 frogs and toads.

On March 24, 1833, the travelers finally reached St. Louis, a dusty frontier boomtown and the center of America's flourishing fur trade. Beyond St. Louis lay vast stretches of unconquered Indian territory. The explorers Lewis and Clark had passed through this region in 1804, and fur traders had been in contact with some western tribes for nearly a century. Yet in 1833, the outside world knew little about the Indians who lived west of the Mississippi River. The land they inhabited seemed as mysterious and remote as the far side of the moon.

In St. Louis, Maximilian and Bodmer met William Clark, co-leader with Meriwether Lewis of their trailblazing expedition to the Pacific and back. General Clark was now Superintendent of Indian Affairs for the western tribes. Anyone wishing to enter Indian territory had to have his permission.

He advised Maximilian to travel up the Missouri River on one of the American Fur Company's new steamboats. An enterprising American painter

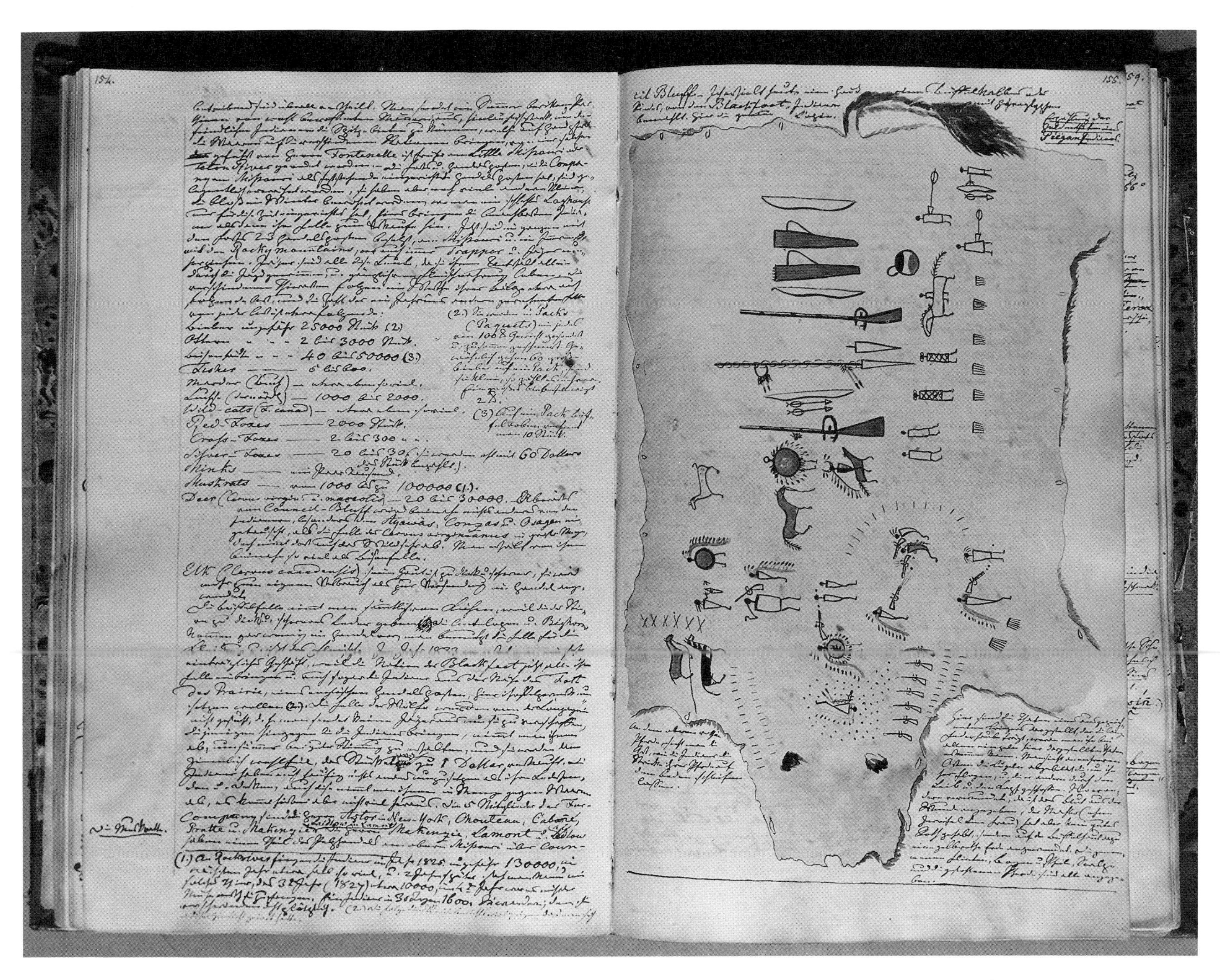

Maximilian often drew pictures in his journal to illustrate his accounts of day-to-day happenings. Here he has sketched a painted Blackfeet hide that records the exploits of a famous warrior.

named George Catlin had done exactly that the year before, venturing as far north as Fort Union. He became the first artist to produce eyewitness portraits of the western Indians and their way of life.

Maximilian and Bodmer planned to venture even farther—to Fort Union and the wilderness beyond. At the fur company's trading posts along the upper Missouri, they would find themselves exactly where they wanted to be—deep in the heart of Indian country.

That summer, a young fur company clerk described the prince and his companions:

"In this year an interesting character in the person of Prince Maximilian from Coblenz on the Rhine made his first appearance on the upper Missouri. . . . He was a man of medium height, rather slender, sans teeth, passionately fond of his pipe, unostentatious, and speaking very broken English. His favorite dress was a white slouch hat, a black velvet coat, rather rusty from long service, and probably the greasiest pair of trousers that ever encased princely legs. The prince was a bachelor and a man of science, and it was in this capacity that he had roamed so far from his ancestral home on the Rhine. He was accompanied by an artist named Boadman [Bodmer] and a servant whose name was, as near as the author has been able to ascertain its spelling, Tritripel [Dreidoppel]."

Two
Adventures on the Upper Missouri

The steamboat *Yellow Stone* had been built by the American Fur Company to carry provisions and the year's supply of trade goods to the company's posts on the Missouri River. Trade with the upper Missouri tribes was thriving. White traders offered guns, tools, kettles, cloth, trinkets, and whiskey in exchange for the Indians' valuable beaver pelts and buffalo hides.

Maximilian, Bodmer, and Dreidoppel were among the passengers when the *Yellow Stone* cast off on the morning of April 10, 1833. The vessel's steam engine hissed and heaved. Its big paddlewheels started to churn. Cannons on shore boomed a salute. And the crowd lining the St. Louis waterfront broke into a lusty cheer as the sidewheeler pulled away from the levee and pointed its prow upstream.

"There were about 100 persons on board," wrote Maximilian, "most of whom were those called *engagés* or *voyageurs,* who are the lowest class of Fur Company employees. Most of them are French Canadians, or descendants of French settlers on the Mississippi and Missouri. They keep big scalping knives in a sheath on their belts. They shouted, fired their guns, and drank."

Ahead on the untamed Missouri lay more than two thousand miles of shifting sandbars, treacherous shallows, and jagged underwater snags that

The steamboat Yellow Stone.

could break the paddles of the wheels or tear into a steamboat's hull. On April 23, Maximilian reported: "Early in the morning a large branch of a tree, lying in the water, forced its way into the cabin, carried away part of the door, and then broke off and was left on the floor. . . . One might have been crushed in bed."

Slowly the *Yellow Stone* made its way north, stopping at each trading post along the way. At some stretches along the river, the boat had to be poled over shallows or pulled off sandbars by sweating *engagés* tugging on long towing ropes from shore. Violent storms swept away deck cargo and smashed one of the smokestacks. Toward dusk every day, the steamer eased into the riverbank and tied up for the night. The Missouri was too dangerous to navigate after dark.

As the travelers entered Sioux territory, they began to see herds of buffalo and antelope and great flocks of wild ducks and geese. Along the banks of the river they passed many Sioux burial scaffolds—platforms above the ground on which the dead, fully dressed and painted and sewn up in blankets and skins, were laid to rest with their weapons and cherished possessions.

Fifty days after leaving St. Louis, the steamboat reached Fort Pierre, near what is now Pierre, South Dakota. This fort was a busy trading post for the Sioux and the end of the line for the *Yellow Stone*. After being loaded with seven thousand buffalo skins and other furs, the steamer turned around and headed back to St. Louis. Maximilian and his companions continued upriver on the *Yellow Stone*'s sister ship, the *Assiniboine*.

In the middle of June they reached Fort Clark, north of present-day Bismarck, North Dakota, where they were greeted by several hundred Mandan and Hidatsa Indians, "all dressed in their finest clothes." A delegation of chiefs came on board, then Maximilian's party went ashore:

"The women and children, in numerous groups, were sitting on the ground. The men, some on horseback, some on foot, gathered around to observe the white strangers. . . . They gazed at us with curiosity, and we conversed with them by signs, but soon proceeded to the fort. . . . A great number of horses were grazing all around. Indians of both sexes and all ages

A Sioux encampment near Fort Pierre. The scaffold on the right holds the remains of a warrior whose body had been brought home from a great distance. Scaffold burial was a common practice among the Sioux and other Plains tribes.

were moving about. We were, at every moment, stopped by them, obliged to shake hands, and let them examine us on all sides."

The next day, as the *Assiniboine* was preparing to leave Fort Clark, a Blackfeet Indian named Kiäsax, or Bear on the Left, came aboard. He had been living among the Hidatsas but now wished to visit his own people at Fort McKenzie, farther up the river. "He was accompanied by his Hidatsa wife, who carried a little child, wrapped in a piece of leather, fastened with straps," wrote Maximilian. "She wept much at parting from her husband."

Kiäsax (Bear on the Left), a Piegan Blackfeet man. He is wearing a striped Navajo blanket and a metal cross around his neck, trade goods from tribes in the Southwest. His wooden flute is decorated with an eagle feather.

When the *Assiniboine* pulled away from shore, a group of Hidatsas on horseback and on foot trailed the steamboat along the river's banks: "The friends and relations of Kiäsax . . . followed the vessel longer than any of the others," Maximilian noted. "They frequently called to him, and nodded farewell, to which Kiäsax answered with a long wooden flute, on which he played a mournful tune."

Fort Union, at the junction of the Missouri and Yellowstone rivers, was as far as a steamboat could navigate. From there, the travelers continued their journey on the *Flora*, a 60-foot-long, flat-bottomed keelboat equipped with a sail and oars. When the *Flora* set sail on July 6 for Fort McKenzie, some 500 miles farther up the Missouri, Maximilian, Bodmer, and Dreidoppel joined 50 fur company employees who had crowded aboard for the trip.

For five weeks the *Flora* pushed its way upstream. When there wasn't enough wind to fill its sail, the crew had to row the vessel with sweeping oars, or push it with long poles, or pull it from shore with strong towing ropes. Straining against the ropes, a gang of 16 or 18 *engagés* would work their way along the river's banks, trudging through mud and thickets, climbing high bluffs, shouting and cursing as they hauled the lumbering keelboat against the swift current. Mosquitoes swarmed in clouds about the boat. Sudden downpours drenched baggage and passengers. Along the way, hunters went ashore in search of game. Soon the open decks of the *Flora* were decorated with the hanging carcasses of deer, elk, and buffalo.

Now the explorers' journey took them through the fantastic rock formations of the *Mauvaises Terres*, or badlands, of the upper Missouri. Here the river cut through miles of eroded limestone hills, resembling strange and picturesque towers and minarets, castles, fortresses, and walls. Bighorn sheep gazed down at them from lofty cliffs. Wolves howled in the distance. Crows flew screaming overhead.

On August 9—four months after leaving St. Louis—Maximilian and his companions finally reached Fort McKenzie, in what is now western Montana. This fort was the American Fur Company's most remote wilderness

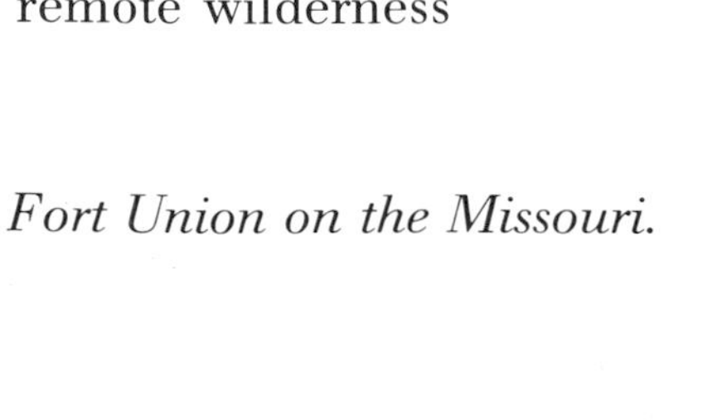

Fort Union on the Missouri.

outpost. It had been built just a year before in an effort to open trade with the powerful Blackfeet, regarded by the whites as the most hostile and warlike Indians in the region.

Outside the walls of the fort, a large encampment of Blackfeet waited for trading to begin. As the *Flora* arrived, the travelers were greeted by hundreds of warriors firing their guns into the air and by throngs of women and children: "Here we were received by the whole population, with the Indian chiefs at their head, with whom we all shook hands."

Maximilian's party spent five weeks at Fort McKenzie at the height of the trading season, and Bodmer had a chance to paint portraits of many tribespeople. "Our residence was besieged all day long by Indians who were attracted by our drawing and writing," reported Maximilian. "They said about Mr. Bodmer, after he had executed a portrait, that he could 'write' well."

In his field journal, Maximilian noted with disapproval that liberal amounts of the white man's firewater were being exchanged for Indian hides and furs. Although it was illegal to give or sell whiskey to the Indians, that law was widely ignored. From the earliest days of the fur trade, alcohol had been a profitable item of trade and a means of taking advantage of the Indians.

"We could see drunken persons everywhere," Maximilian wrote. "Those Indians who had drunk too much whiskey became exceedingly affectionate, shaking hands without end and even embracing and kissing us heartily. They traded their furs for whiskey and clamored for it incessantly."

Alcohol frequently fueled disputes and brawls among Indians and whites alike. One day a fight broke out among some drunken *engagés* at the fort. "Blows were exchanged," wrote Maximilian, "and the example which the whites gave the Indians was not very creditable to them."

Although the Blackfeet had long been hostile to American trappers and traders who trespassed on their hunting grounds, they had recently formed a cautious friendship with the Americans. But they were not on friendly terms

This young Piegan Blackfeet woman needed her husband's permission to pose for a portrait. He agreed in exchange for a gift of red paint and blue beads. Maximilian noted that among the Plains Indians in general, women performed most of the heavy work: "They pitch the tents, chop sod, and lay it around the base of the tents. They cook, cut, gather, and carry home the firewood, tan the hides, and care for the pieces of clothing. In short, they are rather busy."

One of the few children painted by Bodmer, this Piegan Blackfeet girl was living with the Assiniboins. Since the two tribes were enemies, she was probably a war captive being raised by an Assiniboin family. Her hide dress appears to be several sizes too big and is tucked in at the waist.

with their neighbors, the Assiniboins and Crees. On the morning of August 28, a battle erupted:

"At daybreak we were awakened by musket shots. . . . When we entered the courtyard of the fort, all our people were in motion, and some were firing from the roofs. We climbed up and saw the prairie covered with Indians on foot and horseback, who were firing at the fort."

About 600 Assiniboins and Crees had launched a surprise attack against 18 or 20 Indian tents pitched outside the fort, housing Blackfeet who had been singing and drinking the night before. The attackers had slashed the tents with knives and fired guns and arrows at the slumbering Blackfeet, who were roused from their sleep to meet their death. From his vantage point on the roof, Maximilian saw four women and several children lying dead near the fort and many others who were wounded:

"In the fort itself all was confusion. . . . Mr. Mitchell and Berger, the interpreter, were employed in admitting the Blackfeet women and children to the fort when [an Assiniboin], with his bow bent, appeared before the gate and exclaimed, 'White man, make room, I will shoot these enemies!' This showed that the attack was not directed against the whites, but only against the Blackfeet."

Reinforcements arrived from a Blackfeet encampment a few miles away: "They came galloping in groups, their horses covered with foam . . . with all kinds of ornaments and arms, bows and quivers on their backs, guns in their hands, furnished with their medicine bundles, with feathers on their heads . . . and carrying shields adorned with feathers and pieces of colored cloth. A truly original sight! Many of them immediately galloped over the hill [in pursuit of the enemy], whipping their tired horses, shouting, singing, and uttering war-whoops. . . .

"As the Indians near the fort believed themselves to be now quite safe, they carried the wounded into their leather tents, which were damaged and pierced through and through by the enemy's musket shells. Many dead horses and dogs were lying about, and the crying and lamenting never ceased."

Assiniboin and Cree warriors attack a small encampment of Blackfeet outside the Fort McKenzie stockade. Bodmer watched the battle from inside the fort. This engraving was made after he returned to Europe.

A Blackfeet warrior on horseback.

After the battle, a Blackfeet chief named Distant Bear announced that no bullet had touched him, and that his good fortune was due to the magical protection he had gained from the portrait Bodmer had painted of him a few days earlier. "It was striking that all whom we had sketched had neither been wounded nor killed," Maximilian noted. After that, Bodmer's portraits were pronounced "good medicine." Warriors who earlier had been reluctant to pose now insisted that the artist paint their picture.

Maximilian had planned to travel as far west as the Rocky Mountains, but hostilities among the region's tribes now made such a journey seem far too dangerous. He decided instead to head back down the river to Fort Clark and spend the winter among the Mandans and Hidatsas, whom he and his companions had visited briefly on their way north. Both tribes were known to be friendly.

On September 14, Maximilian, Bodmer, and Dreidoppel boarded a small oar-powered Mackinaw boat, built especially for them at Fort McKenzie. The vessel was loaded with crates containing hundreds of Indian artifacts and natural history specimens that the prince had collected, and with cages holding two tame bears he had acquired. Accompanied by a crew of four French-Canadian *engagés*, the travelers prepared to float a thousand miles down the river, living off the land until they reached Fort Clark.

Three

The People of the First Man

The voyage back down the Missouri went quickly. Carried by the swift river current, the prince and his companions glided noiselessly through the wilderness in their Mackinaw boat. They swept past herds of buffalo and elk along the river's banks. Wild geese, swans, and cranes passed overhead, on their way south. During the two-week return trip to Fort Union, the travelers did not see another human being.

The boat was scarcely big enough to hold them all—the three passengers, the four crew members, and Maximilian's two tame bears. The bears' cages sat atop the cargo in the center of the vessel, making it impossible to pass from bow to stern. At dusk, when the travelers pulled over to the river's bank for the night, they would go ashore and spread their blankets under the stars. There was no room to sleep on board.

After a month's layover at Fort Union, they headed downstream again, this time with a crew of five. On the afternoon of November 8, rounding a bend, "We saw the Mandan village of Mih-Tutta-Hang-Kusch and, at no great distance beyond it, Fort Clark, which we reached at four o'clock. We were welcomed on shore by Mr. Kipp, the director and clerk of the fur company, who led us to his house."

Traveling downriver from Fort Union to Fort Clark, Maximilian's party stops for an evening bivouac on the banks of the Missouri. The cages holding the prince's tame bears can be seen in the stern of the Mackinaw boat.

Mih-Tutta-Hang-Kusch, the principal Mandan village.

Mih-Tutta-Hang-Kusch stood high on a windswept bluff overlooking the Missouri. Down below, women were ferrying firewood across the river in tublike, buffalo-skin bullboats. Fort Clark, surrounded by its log stockade, stood 300 paces downstream from the Indian village.

The Mandans led a more settled life than most other Plains Indians. Like their neighbors, the Hidatsas and Arikaras, they lived in permanent villages of earth and timber lodges. They depended as much on farming and trading as they did on hunting.

The men hunted buffalo and other game. The women worked the land, raising corn, beans, pumpkins, and squash in fertile floodplain gardens along the banks of the Missouri. On hunting expeditions the villagers used tipis, but when the hunt ended, they returned home to their earth-lodge villages.

These villages on the upper Missouri had long been important trading centers. The villagers traded produce from their gardens to nomadic tribes for dried meat, dressed hides, and other items in short supply. Because of their strategic location, the Mandans became prosperous middlemen in a vast

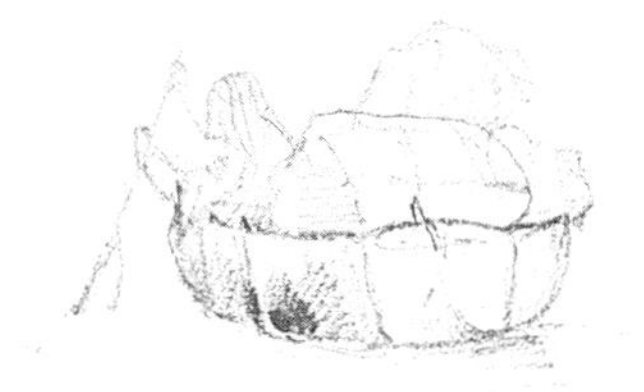

Rowing a bullboat.

trade network that linked tribes as far away as Canada, the Pacific Coast, and the Southwest. Eventually the big fur trading companies sent a few white men to live among the Mandans and Hidatsas and act as company agents.

Fort Clark had been built in 1831 as an American Fur Company trading post. It was staffed by a black cook and about a dozen white employees, including a carpenter, a blacksmith, and interpreters for both the Mandan and Sioux languages. Several of these men had Indian wives. James Kipp, the director of the fort, was married to the daughter of a prominent Mandan family. He spoke Mandan fluently.

Since the fort was already crowded when Maximilian's party arrived, Kipp ordered the construction of a new building to house the three guests. Meanwhile, they doubled up with Kipp's own family.

From the moment the Europeans arrived, they attracted plenty of attention. Dozens of curious Mandans and Hidatsas came to meet the visitors at their temporary quarters at Kipp's house. "They were much pleased with Mr. Bodmer's drawings, and asked us many questions about their enemies, the Blackfeet," Maximilian reported.

One regular visitor was a Mandan elder named Dipauch, or Broken Arm, "who came to tell me all the legends and traditions, as well as the religious views of his people—conversations which interested me much, and which frequently lasted till late at night. Among his audience were several young people, who sat listening with the most riveted attention . . . while Mr. Kipp, with great patience, performed the office of interpreter."

At one time, Maximilian was told, the Mandans had been a much bigger tribe, inhabiting as many as 13 separate villages. Their population had been greatly reduced by a terrible smallpox epidemic during the 1780s, and afterward by the unrelenting attacks of Sioux raiding parties. To protect themselves, they had gathered all their people into two villages—Mih-Tutta-Hang-Kusch, near Fort Clark, and Ruhptare, about three miles up the river. Fifteen miles farther north were the three villages of their friends and allies, the Hidatsas, all situated on the Knife River near its junction with the Missouri.

Each of these communities was made up of a main summer village and a temporary winter one. The people spent most of the year in their summer

Carrying a bullboat.

villages, which stood on bluffs high above the river. There the lodges were safe from spring floods and could be readily defended.

In the winter, the people sought protection along the river's wooded banks, where smaller lodges, nestled among the trees, were sheltered from the winds. Firewood was close at hand here. Horses could survive on the bark of trees when storms kept them away from the prairie. The villagers spent three or four of the year's coldest months in their winter quarters. In spring, when melting snows caused the Missouri to rise, they returned to their summer homes.

Maximilian and Bodmer visited the summer village of Mih-Tutta-Hang-Kusch soon after they arrived at Fort Clark. As they walked from the fort to the village, the barking of family dogs signaled their approach. About 65 large, dome-shaped lodges, or houses, were clustered close together—so close, it was sometimes difficult to pass between them. A stranger could easily lose his way, as in a maze. Meat and corn were hanging on drying racks outside each lodge, and hides were stretched for tanning. People sat on the sloping roofs of their lodges, chatting with one another, shouting down to friends, and watching the passing crowd.

At the heart of the village the visitors found a big open plaza, about 150 feet across. The great medicine lodge, where important rituals and ceremonies took place, faced the plaza, along with lodges occupied by the most influential families in Mih-Tutta-Hang-Kusch.

Standing by itself in the middle of the plaza was the Ark of the First Man, a sacred shrine. According to Mandan belief, the First Man was a powerful spirit, a divine being. He had been created in the distant past by the Lord of Life, the creator of all things, to act as a mediator between ordinary humans and the countless gods, or spirits, that inhabited the universe. The Mandans called themselves "the People of the First Man."

Once, when a great flood swept over the world, the First Man saved the people by teaching them to build a protective tower, or "ark," that would rise high above the floodwaters. In his honor, every Mandan village had a miniature replica of that mythical tower—a cedar post about five feet high, surrounded by a plank fence.

Another religious symbol stood directly in front of the medicine lodge. It

A sketch of the central plaza of Mih-Tutta-Hang-Kusch shows the Ark of the First Man surrounded by its plank fence (at left), and the tall fur-and-feather wrapped pole with a black painted wooden head, representing Ochkih-Hadda, the spirit of evil (at right). In the background are wooden scaffolds used to dry meat and corn.

was a tall pole wrapped with feathers and fur and topped with a hideous wooden head, painted black. This effigy represented Ochkih-Haddä, an evil spirit who had great influence over humans but was not as powerful as the Lord of Life or the First Man. It was said that anyone who dreamed of Ochkih-Haddah was doomed soon to die.

For the Mandans, as for other Plains Indians, belief in the spirit world was an unquestioned part of everyday life. In their view, everything that existed was spiritual. Every object—plants, rocks, water, air, the sun and moon, animals, humans, the earth itself—had a spirit. No major decision could be reached, no project undertaken, without first seeking the aid and approval of the sacred beings who governed human affairs.

Beyond the village on the open prairie, Maximilian and Bodmer found other religious shrines, but the two men could not always learn their meaning. They also saw many burial scaffolds, where the Mandans laid their dead on platforms above the ground. "The body is first laced up in buffalo robes and a blanket," Maximilian wrote. "The face, painted red, is turned toward the east. . . .

"If you ask a Mandan why they do not deposit their dead in the ground, he answers, 'The Lord of Life has, indeed, told us that we come from the ground, and should return to it again. Yet we have lately begun to lay the bodies of our dead on stages, because we love them, and would weep at the sight of them.' "

After a body had decayed and the platform fallen down, the dead person's bones would be buried on the riverbank. The skull, however, would take its place in a circle of skulls on the open prairie—a shrine where relatives and friends could commune with the spirits of those who had departed.

As the Europeans explored, ice was forming on the river, and the Mandans were getting ready for winter. Every day, people were moving with their horses, dogs, and household goods to their winter village in a sheltered grove of cottonwood and willow trees along the river's banks.

On November 22, Maximilian, Bodmer, and Dreidoppel finally moved into the two-room log house that had been built for them. "The whitewashed walls were still damp, and the constant wind generally filled it with smoke," Maximilian noted. "We were, however, thankful to have space to carry on our labors. . . . The large windows afforded good light for drawing, and we had a couple of small tables and some benches of poplar wood, and three shelves against the walls, on which we spread our blankets and buffalo skins, and rested during the night. The room was floored; the door was furnished with bolts on the inside, and the firewood, covered with frozen snow, was piled up close to the chimney."

This Mandan warrior spent several days and nights fasting and crying out to the spirits at a sacred shrine dedicated to two powerful deities, the Lord of Life and the Old Woman Who Never Dies. In the background, burial scaffolds and other religious shrines are scattered across the prairie.

Four
Three Days with the Hidatsas

No sooner had Maximilian and Bodmer settled in than a caller knocked at their door. It was Toussaint Charbonneau, a wily old French-Canadian trader who had been living among the Hidatsa Indians for more than 30 years. He was a well-known character on the upper Missouri. In 1805 he had joined Lewis and Clark as interpreter and guide for their journey to the Pacific. Sacagewea, the Shoshoni Indian woman who played such an important role in that expedition, was one of his many wives.

Charbonneau was well into his seventies and still vigorous when he introduced himself to Maximilian and Bodmer on November 25, 1833. He invited them to visit a winter village of the Hidatsas, about a day's hike away.

They left the following morning. "We had fine weather and a clear sky, very favorable for our expedition," wrote Maximilian. "At nine o'clock, Bodmer, Charbonneau, and myself set out, on foot, with our double-barreled guns and the necessary ammunition, accompanied by a young Hidatsa warrior."

Following the river north, they hiked for hours "through a desolate plain covered with yellow, withered grass, and broken by gentle hills, where bleached buffalo bones, especially skulls, were scattered about. . . .

"As our feet began to be very painful, we sat down to rest near a stream, now almost dry. . . . I was no longer accustomed to such journeys on foot. I had asked Mr. Kipp for horses for this journey, but there were none in the fort at that time. Our European boots and shoes had wounded our feet, and it was with much pain that we climbed the rather steep hills which now and again came nearer to the river. I obtained from Charbonneau a pair of Indian shoes, in which I found it easier to walk, but the thorns of the cactus, which grew on the hills, pierced through them, and caused me pain in another way."

After a tiring nine-hour trek, they saw the Hidatsa village up ahead, nestled in a grove of trees on the banks of the Knife River: "The scenes which are inseparable from the dwellings of the Indians soon appeared. Slender young men, galloping without saddle, were driving their horses home from the pasture. Women were cutting or carrying wood, and the like. A young Indian joined us, who immediately offered, out of politeness, to carry my gun, which I did not accept. He was an Arikara, who had been captured as a child by the Hidatsas—a good-tempered, well-behaved young man."

It was nearly nightfall when the travelers reached the village. Passing between earth lodges, they made their way to the log house belonging to Joseph Dougherty, another fur trader who lived among the Hidatsas. Dougherty gave them a warm welcome. After such a fatiguing journey, they were glad to rest their weary limbs before a blazing fire.

They didn't rest for long, though. Hidatsa scouts had spotted a herd of buffalo nearby, and a hunting party would give chase the next day. To ask the blessings of the spirits and ensure the success of the hunt, the tribe was holding a medicine feast that evening. "Notwithstanding the pain I suffered in walking," wrote Maximilian, "the prospect of witnessing so novel a scene was so exciting that we immediately set out about seven o'clock in the evening to see the Indian ceremony, which was organized by the women."

The ceremony took place in a large, open arena enclosed by a 12-foot-high reed fence. By the time the visitors arrived, a crowd had assembled:

"The spectators, especially the women, were seated. The men walked about, some of them handsomely dressed, others quite simply. Children were seated around the fires, which they kept alive by throwing in twigs of willow trees."

Charbonneau introduced his guests. Then the ceremony began. Six elderly men appeared at the entrance to the open-air medicine lodge. They had been chosen by the hunters to represent buffalo bulls. Each elder held in his right hand a long medicine stick decorated with black feathers at the top, bells at the bottom, and small bundles of buffalo-calf hooves in between. In his left hand he held a battle-ax or a war club. Two of the men carried a badger-skin drum.

Standing at the entrance, the elders rattled their medicine sticks, sang, "and imitated, with great perfection, the hoarse voice of the buffalo bull." Following them was a tall man wearing a fur-trimmed cap—"because he had been formerly scalped in a battle." He was the director of the ceremony and the leader of the six old bulls, who now entered the arena and took seats near the fence, behind one of the fires.

Several young men were carrying around dishes of boiled corn and beans, which they placed before the guests. Each person would taste a little, then pass the dish along. At the same time, empty dishes were brought and placed at the guests' feet. Maximilian didn't understand the reason for this, so he watched his neighbor, a chief named Yellow Bear:

"As soon as the provision bearer—a tall, handsome, very robust, and broad-shouldered man, wearing only his breech-cloth, ornamented at the back with long tufts of hair—came to take away one of these empty dishes, the old chief held his hands before his face, sang, and made a long speech, which seemed to be a prayer uttered in a low tone of voice, and then gave him the dish. These speeches contained good wishes for success in hunting the buffalo, and in war. They called upon the heavenly powers to favor the hunters and the warriors."

A winter village of the Hidatsas.

Addíh-Hiddísch (Maker of Roads), a Hidatsa chief. The tattoos on his arms, hands, and chest, embellished with red paint, symbolize his many war exploits. He wears a European hat, decorated with a coup feather, and a silver peace medal around his neck, a gift from the American government. Hanging from the end of his war hatchet is a scalp stretched on a circular frame.

Péhriska-Rúhpa (Two Ravens), a Hidatsa man. He is wearing his finest ceremonial attire and holding an enormous medicine pipe. His necklace is made of grizzly bear claws. Two Ravens took great pride in his appearance. He spent a long time preparing himself whenever he posed for Bodmer. Another portrait of this dignitary is on page 69.

Now when the empty dishes were placed before Maximilian and Bodmer, they knew exactly what to do: "We also expressed good wishes in the English and German languages, which the Indians guessed from our motions, though they could not understand our words. If our speech was lengthy, they were especially pleased."

When the meal was finished, the hunters prepared the ceremonial tobacco pipes, which they offered first to the elders and the visitors: "They presented the mouthpiece of the pipe to us in succession, going from right to left. We each took a few whiffs, uttered, as before, a wish or prayer, and passed the pipe to our neighbors."

The six buffalo bulls were sitting behind the fire, singing and rattling their medicine sticks as one of them beat the badger-skin drum. After a while they all stood up, bent forward, and danced—leaping as high as they could with both feet together as they continued to sing, rattle their sticks, and beat time on the drum. When they had danced for some time, they resumed their seats.

Maximilian was impressed by the scene: "The great number of red men, in a variety of costumes, the singing, dancing, drum-beating, etc., while the lofty trees of the forest, illuminated by the fires, spread their branches against the dark sky, formed a scene so striking and original, I much regretted the impracticality of making a sketch of it on the spot."

Maximilian and Bodmer spent three days at the Hidatsa village. They visited Chief Yellow Bear in his earth lodge and watched as he sat on a leather bench and painted a buffalo robe with symbolic figures in vermillion and black. His colors stood beside him, ready mixed, in old pieces of pottery, and he applied them to the robe with sharp pointed sticks. "The robe was ornamented with the symbols of valuable presents which he had made, and which had gained Yellow Bear much reputation, and made him a man of distinction," wrote Maximilian.

Generosity was a virtue greatly admired by both the Hidatsas and Mandans. To gain influence and respect, it was important to give presents. When

Yellow Bear wore his painted robe in public, it would be a walking advertisement of his high standing in the community.

Outside his lodge, the village presented a busy and animated scene. The men spent much of their time playing games or watching others play and betting on the outcome. The women were constantly at work, preparing food, carrying firewood, making clothes, tanning buffalo robes. Around dusk they would quit working, gather in groups, and amuse themselves with games of their own.

The visitors watched some young men play the popular hoop-and-pole game. Two players ran along next to each other and tried to hit a leather-laced hoop rolled on the ground or thrown into the air, by hurling long poles at it. Women played a game with a large leather ball, tossing and catching it with their foot. The idea was to keep the ball in the air as long as possible. Children shouted and chased one another beside the frozen Knife River. They slid down snow-covered banks and across the ice in sleds made from buffalo backbones with some of the ribs attached.

Sketches of popular games.

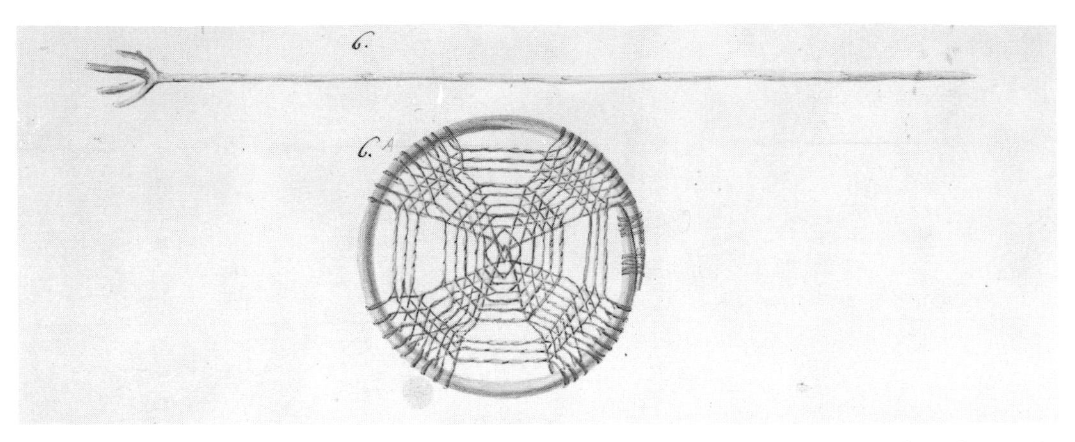

Mandan or Hidatsa hoop and pole. The score depended on exactly where the pole pierced the network of leather thongs.

In the evening, villagers wrapped in warm buffalo robes would sit on their lodge roofs and chat. Young people strolled arm in arm and called on their friends. There was no drinking here—the Hidatsas and Mandans did not touch alcohol—but there was plenty of merriment. The visitors heard "a great deal of noise, shrieking and singing in the village and the surrounding woods."

The Hidatsas struck Maximilian as "the tallest and best-formed Indians on the Missouri." Some of the men were "very handsome . . . strong muscular figures with expressive faces, often nicely painted and adorned. . . . Among the young women we observed some who were very pretty. The white of their sparkling hazel eyes formed a striking contrast to their vermillion faces."

Before leaving, Maximilian and Bodmer had a chance to see another ceremony, the women's corn dance, intended to ensure a bountiful corn crop

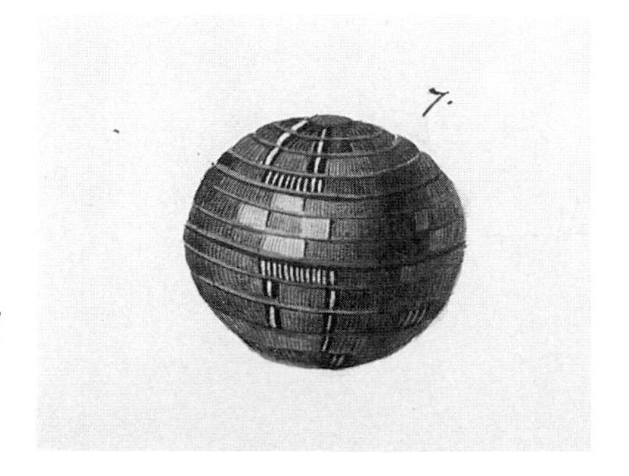

Mandan or Hidatsa leather ball, embroidered with dyed porcupine quills.

the following year. The dance took place in a lodge crowded with spectators. Several musicians were pounding drums, shaking rattles, and singing. A tall medicine woman, wearing a long fringed robe of yellow leather, was standing in the center of the lodge when the Europeans arrived. They were told that she would perform a magical feat: she would conjure up an ear of corn from inside her body, then make it disappear.

The drumbeats, rattling, and singing grew louder. Four other women stepped forward and began to dance, keeping time to the quick beat of the drums: "The medicine woman danced alone by the fire, to which she sometimes put her hands, and then laid them upon her face. At length she began to totter, to move her arms backwards and forwards, and to shake violently. Now, as she threw her head backwards, we saw the top of a white ear of corn fill her mouth and gradually come forward, while her contortions greatly increased.

Bodmer made this unfinished watercolor sketch during his stay at the Hidatsa winter village.

"When the ear of corn was half out of her mouth, the dancer seemed ready to sink down when another woman advanced, laid hold of her and seated her on the ground. Here, supported by her companion, she fell into convulsions, and the music became overpoweringly violent. Other women brushed the arm and breast of the performer with bunches of wormwood, and the ear of corn gradually disappeared. With that, the medicine woman rose, danced twice around the lodge, and was succeeded by another female."

In his journal, Maximilian called the medicine woman a "juggler"—someone who performs tricks. Although he could not explain what he had seen, he felt that she was using sleight of hand to fool her audience. He reported that many others that night "pretended they had some sort of animal in their stomach; some a buffalo calf, others a deer, etc. The scalped man told us that he had a buffalo calf in his left shoulder, and often felt it kick. Another, who pretended that he had three live lizards in his inside, complained to Charbonneau that these animals gave him pain."

Maximilian believed that these people were "pretending." The Indians themselves may have felt that they had the living *spirits* of those animals within themselves. For to them, the spirit world was as real as their own bodies.

Five
Winter

When Maximilian and Bodmer returned to Fort Clark, the Mandans' summer village was practically deserted. Families had blocked the doorways to their lodges with bundles of thorns. They had moved to their tree-sheltered winter village on the river's banks.

That winter was one of the worst in memory. And the log house that had been built so hastily for Maximilian and his companions turned out to be drafty and cold. Frost cracked the plaster between the logs, "so that the bleak wind penetrated on all sides."

By December, the countryside around Fort Clark was buried in snow. Temperatures were plunging. "It was so cold in our quarters that, notwithstanding a good fire, we were unable to work," reported Maximilian. "As Gautier, an old *engagé* was bringing wood into the room, and the door remained open a short time, Mr. Bodmer's colors and brushes froze, so that he could not use them without hot water. Writing, too, was very difficult, because our ink was congealed. And while the side of our bodies which was turned to the fire was half roasted, the other was quite benumbed, and we were often forced to rise in order to warm ourselves. The cook had his ears frost-bitten in going to fetch water. . . .

C. Bodmer

"January set in with increasing cold, which at eight o'clock in the morning was 9 degrees below zero Fahrenheit, and on the 2nd at the same hour, 24 degrees below zero. On the 3rd the mercury sank into the ball and was frozen. . . . The horizon was hazy; the river smoked; neither man nor animal was to be seen."

Bitter cold wasn't the only hardship. As the winds howled and the snow crackled across the prairie, food supplies were running dangerously low. Game was hard to find that winter. Indian hunting parties went out on the coldest days and brought back buffalo meat for their families, but the Fort Clark hunters didn't do as well. A list kept by Maximilian suggests that they shot fewer than a dozen buffalo all winter long, and not much else. "As we now had no meat," he wrote on December 28, "our breakfast consisted of coffee and corn bread, and our dinner of corn bread and bean soup."

Besides running out of meat, they exhausted their stock of tallow, or animal fat, and could no longer make candles. After that, "We were obliged to content ourselves with the light of the fire."

Another worry was the threat of harassment and attack by hostile Indians. One day, Maximilian and Bodmer hiked from Fort Clark to the Mandans' winter village, accompanied by James Kipp, his family, and several Mandan warriors: "We were all well armed, because it was said that a band of hostile Indians had been seen among the prairie hills on the preceding day. . . . We passed, at a rapid rate, through the prairie, along the Missouri, then below the hills. And I cannot deny that, in the valleys and ravines, our

In this winter scene, Fort Clark (on the left) and Mih-Tutta-Hang-Kusch are viewed from the eastern bank of the frozen Missouri. The men, women, and child in the foreground are wrapped tightly in buffalo robes, while the horse and dog brace themselves against the bitter cold.

whole company looked anxiously to the right and left to see whether any enemies would appear from their ambush. We had to pass a narrow gorge behind a thick copse, where many Indians had been killed by their enemies."

At the end of December, Maximilian learned that a raiding party of Yanktonan Sioux had stolen some horses from the Mandans. "This was the fourth time that these Indians had broken the peace concluded in the preceding September," he reported. "The Mandans were so incensed at their treachery that they were disposed to go to war again."

The Assiniboins caused trouble all winter long too. When a group of Assiniboin raiders stole three horses from a Hidatsa lodge one February night, 150 Hidatsa warriors galloped off in pursuit. They overtook the raiders, found one of them asleep, woke him with whips, and killed him on the spot.

Despite the harsh weather, outdoor activity never stopped. The frozen river became a busy thoroughfare. "The Indians are constantly going back and forth from their winter to their summer villages, and to the fort," wrote Maximilian. "Men, women, children, and dogs dragging little sleds are seen on the river all day long."

Thanks to the respected Mandan elder, Broken Arm, Bodmer had a chance to study the interior of a Mandan earth lodge. When most Mandans moved to their temporary winter dwellings, Broken Arm and his family stayed in their summer lodge a short walk from Fort Clark, so that Bodmer could visit them every day and make detailed sketches of the way they lived.

Their home was more spacious and comfortable than any of the log buildings at Fort Clark. The lodge had a sturdy timber framework covered with a dense matting of willow twigs and dry grass. Covering the matting was a thick waterproof layer of hard-packed earth, providing an interior that was cool in summer and cozy in winter.

Inside, there was plenty of room for Broken Arm's large household. Family members and guests sat on buffalo robes spread around the central fire pit, which measured about five feet across and was curbed with stone.

Directly above the fire pit, a large opening in the roof served as both a skylight and a vent for smoke. To keep rain out during storms, the Indians propped an old bullboat on its paddle over the roof opening.

The family's boxlike leather beds were arranged along the walls of the lodge. Each bed, Maximilian noted, was "a large square case made of parchment or skins, with a square entrance. They are large enough to hold several

The entrance to an earth lodge was protected from the weather by a covered passageway with a leather door. Scaffolds for drying meat and vegetables stood outside each lodge, and people often relaxed on the sloping roofs.

Inside a family lodge, the occupants sit on buffalo robes beneath the central skylight, surrounded by their dogs, horses, and useful possessions. A wooden paddle used to propel bullboats leans against the pillar to the left. Hanging above it is a large basket used by women to harvest crops and carry loads on their backs. On the pillars to the right are warriors' weapons and ceremonial gear, including lances with sharp metal blades, buffalo-hide shields, and at far right, a buffalo-head mask complete with horns. In the left foreground, on a robe, is a sacred buffalo skull.

persons, who lie very comfortably and warm on skins and blankets." Pillows were made of old tipi skins stuffed with pronghorn antelope hair and scented with sweetgrass.

Hanging from the scaffolding, leaning against posts, and scattered about the floor were lances and shields, baskets and leather pouches, cooking pots and utensils, and all sorts of household and personal goods. One area was set aside for the family's prized buffalo ponies, which were stabled inside to protect them from severe weather and theft.

A typical family lodge measured as much as 60 feet across, with the skylight perhaps 15 feet above the floor. The lodge sheltered an extended family of 20 people or more, including aunts, uncles, and grandparents. The women of the family built, owned, and maintained the lodge, which was passed on to the daughters. Women also owned the gardens, gardening tools, food, dogs, and colts. Men lived in the household of their wives, bringing only their clothes, horses, and weapons.

Marriage among the Mandans was arranged by families, though the wishes of the young people were taken into account. A successful warrior might be approached by the families of several marriageable girls. Or his own family might open negotiations, with his consent. If the young couple agreed to marry, the two families would exchange horses and other gifts. Then the young man would move into the bride's family lodge, and the marriage would be considered complete.

Marriage to the eldest daughter of a household gave a man the right to marry her younger sisters, too. If he was rich enough to afford several wives, he might do so. However, many men could not afford, or did not wish, more than one wife. "The number of wives varies," Maximilian reported. "They seldom have more than four, and, in general, only one."

Although the lodge itself was owned by the women, the bride's father was considered the head of the household. "Everything depends on him," Maximilian explained, "and is done on his account, and for him. If game is killed, the flesh is first presented to him, and so on."

Like other Plains tribes, the Mandans and Hidatsas looked upon marriage as a bond mainly between families rather than individuals. Even so, there was no lack of romance in their lives. Young men would court a girl when she was out fetching water or firewood, or they would try to attract attention at night by playing melodies of love and longing on their flutes.

A favorite Hidatsa story told of a young woman who heard that her sweetheart had been crippled on a raid. At his own request, he had been abandoned by his companions. When the news reached her, she at once set forth to find him. Braving all dangers, she traveled across hostile territory, found her lover, and with the help of her brother-in-law, who had stayed with the crippled warrior, rescued him.

February brought a welcome break in the cold spell. At the beginning of the month, temperatures rose and a complete thaw set in. "Large tracts of land were wholly free from the snow, which was fast melting away, and only the hills were partly covered," Maximilian wrote. "The ravens and magpies flew about the prairie in search of food."

As the mild weather continued, ice on the Missouri was melting. Fearing that the ice would break up early and the river would rise and flood, the Mandans began to move from their winter dwellings on the river's bank back to their summer lodges high above the Missouri.

Carrying loads.

As usual, the men carried their weapons while the women carried just about everything else. Maximilian was amazed by the heavy burdens that Indian women were able to bear. A woman would tie together a bundle of firewood, then lie on her back on top of the bundle. After the load was secured by a strap slung across her forehead or chest, another woman would raise her to her feet until she was able to stand upright, lean forward, and start walking with the load.

By the middle of February, the winter village stood deserted. Then the mercury plunged again.

At daybreak on February 24, Maximilian noted that the temperature was 26 degrees below zero: "In our apartments everything fluid was frozen, and the quilts on the beds were covered with hoar frost."

Crossing the frozen Missouri with a dog sled. Dogs rather than horses were used as draft animals because they could run over snow or ice without breaking the crust.

Mandeh-Pahchu (Eagle's Beak), a Mandan man. Maximilian commented on the elaborate clothing worn by Plains Indian men and the care that they lavished on their appearance. This young man has adorned his hair with bands of fur, a heavy blue-and-white beaded bangle, and hair-bows with long strings of blue beads and white dentalium shells, tipped with strips of ermine fur. His square earrings, three in one ear, appear to be made of abalone shell. He wears two bead necklaces and carries a flute decorated with otter fur.

Six

Kawakapuska

All winter long, a steady procession of Mandans and Hidatsas called on Maximilian and Bodmer in their chilly quarters. Warriors, elders, and chiefs posed patiently for hours as Bodmer, his fingers stiff with cold, painted their portraits. To entertain them, he would wind up the ornate music box he had brought with him from Switzerland.

Maximilian sat in a corner of the room and asked questions. With the help of James Kipp as interpreter and his own growing knowledge of sign language, he interviewed his guests until late in the night, filling notebook after notebook with "exact information" on every phase of Mandan and Hidatsa life.

Bodmer worked carefully and methodically. Usually he made several sketches of a subject before he was ready to apply his colors. He always started with the face—which was, for him, the key to an individual's personality. He also spent a great deal of time depicting every small detail of Indian clothing, hair style, and personal ornamentation.

One young man became angry when he learned that other warriors had been pictured in their finest clothing, while he had been dressed plainly when he posed. He indignantly demanded that Bodmer destroy his portrait and paint another.

The traditional pictograph on this painted buffalo robe portrays the battle exploits of a famous Hidatsa warrior.

Bodmer's realistic style of painting was very different from traditional Plains Indian pictographs, or picture writing. When an Indian artist painted pictographs on the smooth surface of a buffalo robe, he used simplified stick figures as a kind of pictorial shorthand. He was more interested in recording important events than in picturing people and animals realistically. Bodmer's ability to create lifelike images with his watercolors seemed magical to the Indians who watched him work. When they recognized a likeness, they would often burst into applause. The Mandans called him Kawakapuska—The One Who Makes Pictures.

That winter, Bodmer and Maximilian developed close friendships with two Mandans in particular—the celebrated chief Mató-Tópe, or Four Bears, and the young warrior Síh-Chidä, or Yellow Feather. These two Indians visited the Europeans often. Sometimes they stayed overnight, sleeping on the floor in front of the fireplace.

"Yellow Feather slept again in our room," wrote Maximilian. "After he undressed, he lay down on his [buffalo] robe and made a speech, something like a prayer, to the Lord of Life, from which we understood a few things. He said, among other things, may the Lord of Life send them buffalo, in order to save them from hunger. He spoke in a swift, low voice and without making any gestures."

Síh-Chidä (Yellow Feather), one of Maximilian and Bodmer's closest friends. When he posed for this portrait, he was wearing the same popular style of beaded hair bows as Eagle's Beak (page 46). His heel trailers, otter fur lined with red cloth, represent battle exploits.

The Europeans grew especially fond of this tall, twenty-five-year-old warrior "who became one of our best friends, and visited us almost daily. He was very polished in his manners. . . . He never made demands by asking for anything. As soon as dinner was served he withdrew, though he was not rich, and did not even possess a horse."

Yellow Feather did own some expensive clothes, however. When he posed for his portrait, he was dressed in the height of fashion. He wore a fine buffalo robe, an otter-skin shawl draped around his neck, and strings of rare dentalium shells in his hair.

Fascinated by Bodmer's paintings, Yellow Feather asked the artist to paint a picture of a bird on his war shield. Then he asked for art supplies, so he could try his own hand at the white man's way of painting.

He went about it by following the same approach he had watched Bodmer use—first making a sketch, then adding the colors. Yellow Feather painted portraits of Bodmer, Maximilian, some of his Indian friends, and himself. Instead of simplified stick figures, he made an effort to draw realistic, fully clothed human figures, with carefully rendered eyes and other facial details.

The Europeans' other good friend, Four Bears, ranked as the leading warrior chief of the Mandans. He was admired for his daring and bravery in battle. While he boasted the best war record of any man in his tribe, he also claimed honors as a statesman. More than once, Four Bears had persuaded his people to avoid hostilities and make peace with their enemies. On one occasion, he risked his life to escort an Assiniboin peace delegation to Mih-Tutta-Hang-Kusch through a hail of arrows and bullets.

The chief took great pleasure in teaching Maximilian some words of the Mandan language. He was a valuable source of information about his people's customs. Maximilian described him as an "eminent man . . . being not only a distinguished warrior, but possessing many fine and noble traits of character."

Four Bears often brought friends to meet the Europeans and to pose for portraits. Maximilian noted that he was always "handsomely attired" when

Yellow Feather painted this self-portrait using paper, pencils, and watercolors given to him by Bodmer. He pictured himself on horseback wearing a long red military coat and the feathered war bonnet belonging to his friend Four Bears (see page 77). He is armed with a shield, a ceremonial lance, and a rifle.

Mató-Tópe (Four Bears) posed for Bodmer wearing his war paint. The six colored wooden sticks in his hair represent gunshot wounds, while the split turkey feather stands for an arrow wound. The carved and painted wooden knife above his ear is a facsimile of the weapon he wrested from a Cheyenne chief in hand-to-hand combat. The yellow hand painted on his chest shows that he has captured prisoners, while the barred stripes across his arm indicate other military coups.

he visited: "This chief, indeed, had on a different outfit almost every time he came to see us."

Bodmer painted two pictures of Four Bears. One of these shows the chief with tomahawk in hand, wearing little else but his war paint. Each painted mark on his body, every object in his hair and on his person, signifies an act of valor. The second portrait (page 77) shows Four Bears dressed in full ceremonial regalia, including an impressive headdress. In that picture, symbols of his valiant deeds and his war wounds are painted on his sheepskin shirt. Like a general with a chestful of medals, the chief wore his battle regalia proudly.

Like other Plains tribes, the Mandans were a warrior society. Success in battle was the key to gaining honor and respect within the tribe. An ambitious young man who wanted to earn a reputation for himself would try to get up a war party. To do this, he had to give feasts for the warriors he wished to recruit. And he had to convince them that his undertaking had the support of the spirits.

If he managed to organize a war party, and if the warriors brought home enemy scalps and horses without losing any of their own men, then the expedition was counted a success. Back in the village, the young leader was expected to show his generosity by giving away any horses or loot he had captured—but his career as an important man in the community was launched.

However, if anyone in his war party was killed, the leader was disgraced. He was said to have "kicked the stone." He could redeem himself only by slashing his own flesh and through an expensive campaign of feasts and gift-giving for the families of the fallen warriors. If the young man organized a second war party and failed again, his dreams of glory were finished.

Four Bears had led many successful war parties in his time. He claimed to have slain no fewer than five enemy chiefs in battle. His most celebrated exploit was his triumph over a Cheyenne chief in hand-to-hand combat—a story he told Maximilian more than once. He was on a scouting expedition with a few Mandan warriors when they encountered four Cheyennes—their

most bitter foes—on horseback. The Cheyenne chief saw that his enemies were on foot and that any combat would be unequal, so he dismounted. Then the two parties attacked.

Four Bears and his opponent fired at each other with their single-shot muskets, missed, then tossed the guns aside. The Cheyenne, a tall, powerful man, drew his knife. Four Bears, who was lighter and more agile, seized his battle-ax. When the Cheyenne attempted to stab Four Bears, the Mandan chief grabbed the blade of the knife, slashing his hand but wresting the weapon away from his enemy, and stabbed him. From that time on, Four Bears wore a painted wooden replica of the knife in his hair, an emblem of that fight.

Like his young friend Yellow Feather, Four Bears was an enthusiastic painter. He depicted his battle with the Cheyenne chief using the white man's art supplies—pencils, paper, and watercolors—and also in the traditional Indian way, by painting a pictograph on a buffalo robe. Afterward, he presented the robe as a gift to his friend Maximilian.

This is Four Bears's own painting of his famous battle with the Cheyenne chief. He is wearing his feathered headdress and brandishing his tomahawk as he grabs for his enemy's knife and slashes his hand. The guns that the two warriors tossed aside are shown at either side of the picture.

A leader of the Mandan Buffalo Bull Society.

Seven

Buffalo Bulls and White Buffalo Cows

One winter morning, Indian drums were heard beating in the distance. Slowly the drummers approached Fort Clark, announcing the arrival of the Ravens:

"The whole company, very gaily and handsomely dressed, soon afterwards entered the fort, followed by a crowd of spectators. About twenty vigorous young men threw off their robes at the entrance. Their bare chests painted and ornamented in the most gaudy manner, they formed a circle in the courtyard of the fort.

"As soon as the drum beats started again, the dancers bent their bodies forward and leaped up with both feet together, holding their guns in their hands, and their fingers on the triggers, as if going to fire. In this manner they danced for about a minute in a circle, then gave a loud shout, and, having rested a little, began to dance again."

The Ravens were one of many ceremonial societies that played an important role in the lives of both Mandans and Hidatsas. There were societies for men and for women of different age groups, each with its special dances and songs, its own emblems, rituals, privileges, and duties. As a person passed through life, he or she could buy membership in these organizations, advancing from one age-graded society to the next.

Maximilian described six men's societies among the Mandans, ranging from the Foolish Dogs for boys to the Black-tailed Deer for older men. The Foolish Dogs was for youngsters from about 10 to 15 years of age. As a badge of membership, each boy wore around his neck a small war whistle made from the wing bone of a wild goose.

When a youngster wanted to join the Foolish Dogs, he would approach one of the members, address him as "Father," and ask if he could buy that member's place in the group. He would say: "Father, I am poor, but I wish to buy from you." In exchange, he would offer valuable gifts, such as blankets, guns, or even horses, which his relatives had agreed to supply. If the place was sold to him, he then had a right to all the privileges and distinctions of the Foolish Dogs, including the songs, dances, and regalia that belonged to that society alone.

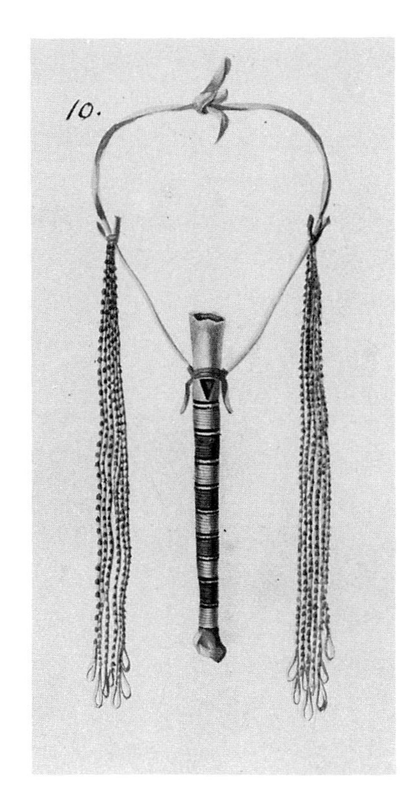

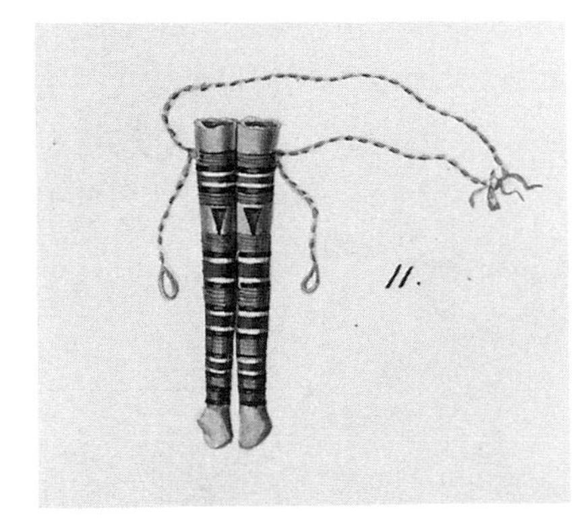

Mandan war whistles. Membership in each men's society was signified by a different kind of ornamental whistle made from the hollow wing bones of geese, swans, or cranes.

Maximilian witnessed one of the dances performed by the Foolish Dogs—a test of a boy's courage and fortitude. He called it the "hot dance":

"A large fire is kindled, and live coals are scattered on the ground, about which the young men dance, quite naked and barefoot. Their hands, with the lower part of their arms, and their feet and ankles, are painted red. A kettle, with meat cut in small pieces, is hung over the fire. When the meat is done they plunge their hands into the boiling water, take out the meat, and eat it, at the risk of scalding themselves. The last comers are the worst off, having to dip their hands the deepest into the boiling water. During the dance they have in their hands their weapons and their rattles."

The boys who bought places in the Foolish Dogs did not join the sellers as members, but replaced them. Those who sold their membership ended all ties to that particular society. They remained a group, however. Together they bought admission to the next age-graded society, the Ravens, for young men up to about 25 years of age. In this way, the original gang of boys would advance from one society to the next, buying admission each step of the way, entering the system of societies as boys and remaining in it until old age.

Moving on to the next-higher society required diplomacy and persuasion. The younger group was eager to advance, while their elders, who were always called their "fathers," made the most of their privileged position. They would agree to give up their beloved songs, dances, and regalia only with the greatest reluctance.

The hopeful buyers would bring valuable gifts to the sellers' ceremonial lodge. They would ask the older men to smoke a pipe with them as a token of good faith. But the sellers would usually object that this first gift offering wasn't enough, so the buyers would go back home to collect more property from their relatives. Eventually the older men would agree to smoke the pipe. But they still acted as though they were doing their juniors a big favor.

The transfer of rights and privileges from the sellers to the buyers was an important occasion. It called for a great feast, paid for by the younger men, lasting many nights. As the sellers enjoyed the feast, they began to teach the buyers the songs, dances, and rituals that were the exclusive property of their society. Many speeches were made, urging the "sons" to follow the example of the distinguished "fathers." Finally the departing members would turn over their ceremonial lances and other insignia to the younger men, who would then parade and dance in public.

A ceremonial society was like a club. A member would spend much of his time at the society's lodge, often eating and sleeping there, enjoying the comradeship of his fellows. Societies also had serious public duties. Each group was responsible for a social function—policing the village, scouting, or planning the hunt.

The most prestigious men's society was the Buffalo Bulls. Its members were seasoned warriors, men in their forties who had earned the respect of their fellows and acquired enough wealth to buy their way through each of the younger societies. They wore bands of buffalo hide across their foreheads, with a pair of horns attached.

Two Buffalo Bulls, recognized for their exceptional bravery, were chosen as leaders by their comrades. During dances and ceremonies, they had the right to put on complete buffalo-head masks with metal-rimmed eye and mouth slits. Wearing such a mask was one of the highest honors that could be accorded a Mandan warrior. These men pledged never to retreat from an enemy, no matter how great the danger.

Mandan women had their own age-graded societies. Girls who belonged to the youngest group, the Society of the Gun, had the right to decorate their hair with eagle's down. The oldest women's group was the Society of the White Buffalo Cow. These women wore special hats made from the hide of the rare and sacred white buffalo.

On Christmas Day of 1833, 17 members of the White Buffalo Cows performed one of their dances at Fort Clark. They were accompanied by two men, musicians with rattles and a drum:

"A stout elderly woman went first. She was wrapped in the hide of a white buffalo cow, and held, in her right arm, a bundle of twigs in the form of a cornucopia, with down feathers at the top, and at the lower end an eagle's

Dance of the Buffalo Bulls Society.

wing and a tin drinking cup. Another woman carried a similar bundle. All these women wore around their heads a piece of white buffalo skin in the form of a hussar's cap, with a plume of owl's or raven's feathers in front, some of which were dyed red. . . .

"The women were uniformly painted. The left cheek and eye were vermillion, and they had two blue spots on the temple near the right eye. All except the first wore painted robes, and two of them only had the hairy side outward. When they had formed a circle the music began in quick time. The men sang, and the women who were dancing responded with loud shrill voices. In their dance they rock from side to side, always remaining in the same spot."

Maximilian and Bodmer saw many dances and ceremonies that winter, but the most haunting was the traditional scalp dance performed by Hidatsa women to celebrate a victory by their warrior husbands. For this ceremony, the wives put on military attire, painted their faces like warriors, carried weapons, and dangled enemy scalps from the ends of long poles.

The scalp dance was performed at Fort Clark one afternoon in February:

"At two o'clock the Hidatsa women arrived in procession, accompanied by many children and some Mandans. Eighteen women, marching two and two in close column, entered the courtyard of the fort, with a short-measured, slow pace. Seven men of the Society of the Dogs, having their faces painted black, or black striped with red, acted as musicians, three of them having drums, and four rattles. They were wrapped in their buffalo robes, and their heads were uncovered and ornamented with the feathers of owls and other birds. The faces of some of the women were painted black, others red, while some were striped black and red. They wore buffalo dresses, or blankets, and the two principal women were wearing white buffalo robes. . . .

"In their arms they carried battle-axes or guns, ornamented with red cloth and short black feathers . . . in short, while performing the dance, the women are outfitted in the military dress and weapons of the warriors. The right wing was headed by the wife of the chief, Itsichaika, who carried in her

Dance of the White Buffalo Cows Society.

hand a long elastic rod. Suspended from the tip of the rod was the scalp of the Assiniboin warrior slain the previous day, topped by a stuffed magpie with outspread wings. Lower down on the same rod hung a second scalp, a lynx skin, and a bunch of feathers. Another woman carried a third scalp on a similar rod.

"The women filed off in a semicircle. The musicians, taking their stand by the left wing, started to play loudly, beating their drums, shaking their rattles, and yelling with all their might. The women began to dance, waddling in short steps, like ducks. The two wings, or horns of the crescent, advanced towards each other, and then receded, at the same time singing in a shrill tone of voice. . . .

"After a while they rested, and then began again, and continued dancing about twenty minutes. The director of the fort now caused tobacco, mirrors, and knives from the company's stores to be thrown as gifts into the middle of the circle. With that, the women once more danced in quick time, the musicians forming themselves into a close body and holding their instruments towards the center. This concluded the festivity."

Maximilian and Bodmer did not get to see the famous Okipa, a four-day religious ceremony held every spring. During this sacred rite, painted and costumed tribe members impersonated spirits from the animal world. Dancers re-created the tribal myth of the creation of the world. And young warriors demonstrated their courage and endurance. They went without food or water for the entire four days, and at the climax of the ceremony, they offered their flesh to the spirits in an agonizing ritual of self-torture.

These warriors skewered the flesh of their arms, chests, and backs with hooks. They were then suspended by rawhide ropes from sacred poles in the ceremonial lodge. Buffalo skulls hooked to their legs increased their weight as they hung. Later they ran about outside the lodge, dragging the heavy skulls behind them, until pain rendered them unconscious or caused them to have visions.

The Okipa was the year's most important religious event. It required weeks of preparation and involved every single person in the village, either as

Scalp dance of the Hidatsa wives.

a performer or a spectator. Maximilian and Bodmer's friend Four Bears was chosen as director of the Okipa for the spring of 1834. Although the ceremony took place after the Europeans had left for home, Four Bears described the ritual to them in vivid detail.

"The wounds that have been inflicted on this occasion heal," wrote Maximilian, "but they remain visible for a lifetime, like thick swollen welts. . . . The buffalo skulls, which these Indians have dragged about with much pain, are preserved in their lodges, where they are everywhere to be seen, to be handed down from the father to the children. Many such skulls are looked upon by them as medicine [magic]. They are kept in the lodges, and sometimes the Indians stroke them, and set food before them."

Bodmer sketched these Hidatsa women when they visited Fort Clark to perform their scalp dance. The musicians with drums and rattles are men.

Eight
The Last Time You Will Hear Me

Early in March, Maximilian was stricken with a mysterious illness. It began as a swelling in one knee. Soon his whole leg was puffed up and horribly black and blue: "A violent fever followed, with great weakness, and having neither medical advice nor suitable remedies, my situation became daily more helpless and distressing, as there was nobody who had any knowledge of this disorder."

Maximilian was too sick to get out of bed, but he continued to receive visitors. And Bodmer continued to paint their portraits. The Hidatsa chief Péhriska-Rúhpa, or Two Ravens, spent several days posing for the artist, dressed in the regalia of the Dog Society.

"When the sitting was over," wrote Maximilian, "Two Ravens always took off his huge feathered cap and rubbed it twice on each side of his head, a charm or precaution which he never neglected. He then seated himself with his friend Four Bears by the fireside, where both of them took up their pipes. Four Bears, however, always turned around first and made everybody in the room sit down.

"During my confinement to bed, I looked forward to the frequent visits of the Indians. And I never neglected to continue my journal, which was often

Péhriska-Rúhpa (Two Ravens) in the regalia of the Hidatsa Dog Society. His elaborate ceremonial headdress of feathers, down, and horsehair was in constant motion as he danced.

very fatiguing due to my constant fever and weakness. Mr. Kipp kindly sent me some new-laid eggs every day, as well as rice, which he had reserved for me, and from which I derived great benefit. The inmates of the fort had nothing to eat but doughy corn bread and corn boiled in water."

At long last, the season's first wild ducks were seen flying north. A few days later the first wild swans arrived. The birds paused in their journey to splash about in the pools of melted snow that were forming in the Mandans' cornfields.

Then Four Bears and Two Ravens went hunting. They returned triumphantly. They had killed five buffalo, and to show their friendship and generosity, they gave some of the meat to Maximilian.

On April 2, the women of Mih-Tutta-Hang-Kusch celebrated the spring corn feast, held every year when the first wild geese returned. Each important Mandan crop was symbolized by a migratory wildfowl: the duck stood for beans, the swan for pumpkins or squash, and the goose for corn. The Mandans regarded these birds as messengers from the Old Woman Who Never Dies, the deity who caused beans, squash, and corn to grow. The arrival of the first migrating geese was a signal to bless the seeds that would be sown for that year's corn crop.

The corn feast was held just outside the village, on the open prairie. Strips of dried meat, along with other gifts, were hung on long horizontal poles above the ground, as sacred offerings to the Old Woman Who Never Dies. Her representatives, the elderly women of the village, gathered around these offerings, holding sticks with ears of corn stuck to one end. Sitting in a circle, they planted the sticks in the ground. Then they performed the sacred corn dance. Afterward, grains of this consecrated corn were mixed with the seed corn to be sown later that spring. In the autumn, the Mandans said, when the geese flew south again, they would return to the Old Woman, carrying with them the gifts that had been offered by the old women of Mih-Tutta-Hang-Kusch.

The corn feast ended at about eleven that morning, but the celebration lasted all day as the entire village welcomed the arrival of spring. Bodmer drew a sketch of the festive scene that day, and Maximilian noted in his journal, "Great numbers of young men were running races, and all was animation about the village."

By now, the ice that had blocked the Missouri's course all winter was beginning to thaw and break up. But Maximilian was sicker than ever: "At the beginning of April I was still in a hopeless condition, and so very ill, that the people who visited me did not think that my life would be prolonged beyond three or, at the most, four days. The cook of the fort, a Negro from St.

This sketch was made during the Mandan women's spring corn feast on the prairie outside Mih-Tutta-Hang-Kusch.

Louis, one day expressed his opinion that my illness must be the scurvy, for he had once witnessed many deaths among the garrison of the fort at Council Bluffs, when several hundred soldiers were carried off in a short time."

The cook offered some advice. At Council Bluffs, he told Maximilian, "at the beginning of spring, they had gathered green herbs in the prairie, especially the small white flowering *Allium reticulatium* [wild onion], with which they had soon cured the sick. I was advised to try this recipe, and the Indian children accordingly furnished me with an abundance of this plant and its bulbs. These were cut up small, like spinach, and I ate lots of them. On the fourth day the swelling of my leg had considerably subsided, and I gained strength daily. The prospect of speedy recovery quite reanimated me, and we carried on with pleasure the preparations for our departure, though I was not yet able to leave my bed."

The river was now free of ice, and the Europeans were anxious to get started on their long journey home. Maximilian's Mackinaw boat was freshly caulked and made ready for the voyage down the Missouri to St. Louis. The open deck was sheltered by a big Indian tent. Then the boat was loaded with crates containing hundreds of specimens and artifacts that Maximilian had collected, ranging from dried plants and stuffed animals to Indian weapons, tools, ornaments, and clothing. Maximilian's two caged bears, which had spent most of the winter quietly hibernating, were the last to be loaded on board.

On April 18, Maximilian, Bodmer, and Dreidoppel exchanged gifts and farewells with the friends they had made, whom they might never see again: "At noon, the boat was loaded. After we had partaken of our last frugal dinner at Fort Clark, we took a cordial farewell of Mr. Kipp, with whom we had passed so long a time in this remote place, and who had done everything for me that was possible. . . . Accompanied by the inhabitants of the fort, and many of our Indian friends, among whom were Four Bears and Two Ravens, all of whom shook hands at parting, we went on board our boat. The weather was favorable, though there was a strong wind from the south-west. Some cannon shots were fired by the fort as a farewell salute, and we glided rapidly down the beautiful stream of the Missouri."

Maximilian was still so weak that he had to be helped aboard the boat at Fort Clark. But his health improved quickly as the big flat-bottomed Mackinaw floated down the river under the warm spring sun. The voyage lasted six weeks, with stopovers at trading posts along the way. On May 27, 13 months after they had started their journey up the Missouri, the travelers reached St. Louis again.

From there, Maximilian, Bodmer, Dreidoppel, and the two bears traveled eastward across the United States by river steamer, canal boat, and overland stagecoach. They stopped to visit Niagara Falls and New York City before sailing for Europe and home on July 16, 1834. They never returned to America again.

In the spring of 1837, another deadly epidemic of smallpox swept up the Missouri River, carried north by passengers aboard the American Fur Company's annual steamboat. The Mandans were the first to be stricken, followed in swift succession by the Hidatsas, the Assiniboins, the Arikaras, the Sioux, and the Blackfeet. By the time the epidemic had run its course, an estimated one out of four Indians along the upper Missouri had died.

The Mandans, hardest hit of all, were virtually destroyed as a tribe. When Maximilian and Bodmer spent the winter with them in 1834, they numbered perhaps 1,600 men, women, and children. By the end of 1837, about 130 Mandans were still alive.

Smallpox had been carried to the New World by early European settlers. The Indians had no natural immunity to this foreign virus, so they succumbed quickly. Because so few whites died, some Indians suspected that the disease had been introduced among them deliberately, or that the whites had a secret remedy which they would not share. Anger against the whites mounted. At Fort Clark, attempts were made to kill Francis Chardon, who had replaced James Kipp as the fort's director.

A Mandan shrine near the burial ground of Mih-Tutta-Hang-Kusch.

The great Mandan chief Four Bears, described by Chardon as "one of our best friends in the village," watched in horror as his people wasted away and perished. He saw his wives and children suffer and die. Then he, too, turned bitterly against the whites. He tried to muster a war party to attack Fort Clark, but by then, there were hardly enough warriors left alive and the chief himself had been stricken with smallpox.

It is said that in his last hours, Four Bears made an impassioned speech, accusing the whites of bringing a shameful and terrifying end to him and his people. The speech has come down to us from Francis Chardon, who kept a journal during that dark plague year. Chardon could not have been present to hear the speech itself, and in any case, he spoke little Mandan. We can never know how accurately he transcribed the chief's last words. But there is little doubt that he conveyed Four Bears's despair and resentment at that time.

Here is the speech in full, just as it was written down by Chardon:

> My friends one and all, listen to what I have to say—Ever since I can remember, I have loved the Whites, I have lived With them ever since I was a Boy, and to the best of my Knowledge, I have never Wronged a White Man, on the Contrary, I have always Protected them from the insults of Others, Which they cannot deny. The 4 Bears never saw a White Man hungry, but what he gave him to eat, Drink, and a Buffaloe skin to sleep on, in time of Need. I was always ready to die for them, Which they cannot deny. I have done everything that a red Skin could do for them, and how have they repaid it! With ingratitude! I have Never called a White Man a Dog, but to day, I do Pronounce them to be a set of Black harted Dogs, they have deceived Me, them that I always considered as Brothers, has turned Out to be My Worst enemies. I have been in Many Battles, and often Wounded, but the Wounds of My enemies I exhalt in, but to day I am Wounded, and by Whom, by those same White Dogs that I have always Considered, and treated as Brothers. I do not fear *Death* my

friends. You know it, but to *die* with my face rotten, that even the Wolves will shrink with horror at seeing Me, and say to themselves, that is the 4 Bears the Friend of the Whites—

Listen well what I have to say, as it will be the last time you will hear Me. think of your Wives, Children, Brothers, Sisters, Friends, and in fact all that you hold dear, are all Dead, or Dying, with their faces all rotten, caused by those dogs the whites, think of all that My friends, and rise all together and Not leave one of them alive. The 4 Bears will act his Part.

Four Bears died that day—July 30, 1837.

Maximilian's account of his journey was published in German in 1839, and later in French and English editions. The book was illustrated by a separate portfolio of engravings made under Karl Bodmer's supervision. Today, through the prince's words and the painter's pictures, we can still share their experience as they visited Indian tribes along the upper Missouri more than a century and a half ago.

"Wonders passed us as in a dream," wrote Maximilian. "They would, perhaps, have left but an indistinct and gradually fading impression, had not the skillful hand of the artist rescued them from oblivion."

Mató-Tópe (Four Bears) in full ceremonial dress.

Bodmer painted this view of distant mountains during his stay at Fort McKenzie.

Afterword

After Prince Maximilian returned to his castle on the Rhine, he spent four years editing his field journals for publication as a book. Karl Bodmer settled in Paris, where he went to work on a series of engravings to illustrate the account.

In the 1830s, it was not possible to reproduce colored paintings on a printing press. Illustrations for book publication were made by printing black-and-white engravings, which could then be colored individually by hand. For Maximilian's book, Bodmer supervised a staff of 20 engravers, who produced 81 copper plate aquatints, based on his original watercolors and sketches. The engravings were published as a separate picture atlas that accompanied the book. Some sets of these black-and-white prints were hand colored.

Travels in the Interior of North America, Maximilian's two-volume account of his expedition, appeared in German-, French-, and English-language editions between 1839 and 1843. Following publication, Bodmer's original paintings and drawings—nearly 400 of them—were sent to the Wied estate on the Rhine for safekeeping.

Maximilian's expedition up the Missouri was his last great adventure. A lifelong bachelor, he shared a small stone house with his brother Charles on the family estate, where he continued to read, study, and write about North America and to add to his natural history collections.

Bodmer stayed on in Paris, where he married and became a fashionable painter of forest landscapes and animal studies, and a popular book and magazine illustrator. He often reminisced about his exciting days in America, but he never again painted an Indian subject.

Over the years, the two men kept in touch. In 1865, they collaborated on one more project, a catalogue of North American reptiles and amphibians, which Bodmer illustrated with engravings. Two years later, in 1867, Maximilian died at the age of 84. Bodmer, stricken with blindness in his last years, died in Paris in 1893. He was also 84. By then, his reputation as an artist had faded, and soon his life's work was all but forgotten.

His North American paintings and drawings remained hidden away in Maximilian's castle for more than a century before they were rediscovered after World War II by a German museum official engaged in research at the Wied family estate. In 1962, the entire collection, along with Maximilian's original journals, diaries, letters, books, and maps, was purchased by the Northern Natural Gas Company, now InterNorth, Inc., and placed on permanent loan with the Joslyn Art Museum in Omaha, Nebraska.

Bodmer's watercolors and Maximilian's written descriptions have come down to us as an unsurpassed portrait of the native peoples who once lived along the upper Missouri. The journals are considered the most complete and reliable eyewitness account ever written of the Mandan and Hidatsa cultures. They have been a standard source for scholars since their first publication. Bodmer ranks as one of the great artists of the American frontier, an inspired portraitist and landscape painter whose works are admired today for both their beauty and their meticulous accuracy.

The Mandans and Hidatsas who befriended Maximilian and Bodmer never fully recovered from the devastating smallpox epidemic of 1837. Those tribes and the neighboring Arikaras were reduced to the point where they could all occupy a single village. With the extermination of the buffalo during the 1860s and 1870s and the steady loss of tribal lands to white settlers, their traditional way of life vanished.

Prince Maximilian in later life.

Karl Bodmer as he appeared in middle life.

The Mandans, Hidatsas, and Arikaras have shared the Fort Berthold Reservation in North Dakota since it was established in 1870. Now known as the Three Affiliated Tribes, they have come to be a single people.

Today they live on their reservation in scattered farms and ranches, and in small communities where neat pastel houses are centered around a community hall, a modern school building, a church or two, and a gleaming water tower. Although the old ways are gone, they are remembered. Youngsters in school study the culture and history of their ancestors, and at tribal powwows, traditional ceremonies are still observed.

If the ghosts of Maximilian and Bodmer could visit the site where the Mandan village of Mih-Tutta-Hang-Kusch once stood, they would find little to remind them of the past. Looking toward the northwest, they would see two huge electric generating plants outlined against the horizon. But if they turned their ghostly heads and listened to the prairie wind, they might hear an Indian flute playing a mournful tune.

Places to Visit

Fort Clark State Historic Site, Mercer County, North Dakota, $7\frac{1}{2}$ miles southeast of Stanton. Sixty miles north of Bismarck, a county road leads to the lonely, windswept bluff once occupied by Fort Clark and the Mandan village of Mih-Tutta-Hang-Kusch. A historical marker at the entrance provides information about the site. From there it is a short walk to the village site, where nearly 100 grass-covered circular depressions indicate the locations of the Mandans' earth lodges. Numbered stakes identify points of interest on a self-guided walking tour that covers the village proper, the central plaza, the fortification ditch, and, 300 paces to the south, the site of Fort Clark. Although the Missouri no longer flows at the base of the bluff (the river's present course is nearly a mile away), a visitor, in imagination, can picture the busy and animated scenes of life that Prince Maximilian and Karl Bodmer witnessed here in the winter of 1833–34. Open during the summer months only. For more information, write to the Historic Sites Division, State Historical Society of North Dakota, North Dakota Heritage Center, Bismarck, ND 58505.

Knife River Indian Villages National Historic Site, Mercer County, North Dakota, just north of Stanton. This is where Hidatsa villages flourished along the Knife River near its junction with the Missouri at the time of Maximilian and Bodmer's visit. Self-guided walking tours lead the visitor through the sites of Big Hidatsa Village and Awatixa Village. A Visitor Center features exhibits and offers informative maps and brochures. Open all year. For more information, write to the Superintendent, RR #1, Box 168, Stanton, ND 58571.

Both of the above sites can be reached via U.S. Highway 83 and State Highway 200A.

Ward Earthlodge Village Historic Site, east of Pioneer Park on Burnt Boat Drive, Bismarck, North Dakota. This site near downtown Bismarck was occupied by the Mandans during the period 1675–1780. It has 43 earth-lodge depressions, enclosed on three sides by a fortification ditch. A trail with interpretive markers leads through the site. Open all year. For more information, write to the Bismarck Parks and Recreation District, 215 N. 6th Street, Bismarck, ND 58501.

North Dakota Heritage Center, State Capitol Grounds, Bismarck, North Dakota. A number of exhibits concerning Native American history and culture are included in this comprehensive state historical museum. Open all year. For more information, write to the State Historical Society of North Dakota, North Dakota Heritage Center, Bismarck, ND 58505.

Joslyn Art Museum, 2200 Dodge Street, Omaha, Nebraska 68102. Most of Bodmer's original North American studies are part of the Joslyn's Bodmer-Maximilian Collection, which also includes Maximilian's original travel diaries, journals, letters, and related memorabilia. Selected watercolors, sketches, and aquatints by Bodmer are always on display at the museum.

List of Illustrations

All works are by Karl Bodmer unless otherwise noted

Bibliography

Maximilian's account of his North American expedition was first published in an English edition in 1843, with a translation by H. Evans Lloyd. The Lloyd translation was reprinted as part of Reuben Gold Thwaites's *Early Western Travels* in 1906. Edited selections from the Lloyd translation were again reprinted in Davis Thomas and Karen Ronnefeldt's *People of the First Man* in 1976. For this book, I have adapted the Lloyd translation to make the account accessible to a contemporary audience of young readers, hopefully retaining the spirit and substance of the nineteenth-century original.

Maximilian, Prince of Wied. *Travels in the Interior of North America, 1832–1834.* Translated by H. Evans Lloyd. London: Ackermann & Co., 1843; reprinted as vols. 22–24 of Reuben Gold Thwaites, *Early Western Travels, 1748–1846.* Cleveland: Arthur H. Clark Co., 1906.

Thomas, Davis, and Karen Ronnefeldt, eds. *People of the First Man: Life Among the Plains Indians in Their Final Days of Glory—The Firsthand Account of Prince Maximilian's Expedition Up the Missouri River, 1833–34.* New York: Dutton, 1976.

Other works on the Maximilian-Bodmer expedition and the Indians of the upper Missouri include:

Ewers, John C., Marsha V. Gallagher, David C. Hunt, and Joseph C. Porter. *Views of a Vanishing Frontier.* A Catalogue to the Exhibition. Omaha: Center for Western Studies/Joslyn Art Museum, 1984.

Goetzmann, William H., David C. Hunt, Marsha V. Gallagher, and William J. Orr. *Karl Bodmer's America.* Lincoln: University of Nebraska Press, 1984.

Goetzmann, William H., and William N. Goetzmann. *The West of the Imagination.* New York: W.W. Norton & Company, 1986.

Hyde, George E. *Indians of the High Plains.* Norman, Okla.: University of Oklahoma Press, 1959.
Lowie, Robert H. *Indians of the Plains.* New York: McGraw-Hill, 1954.
Meyer, Roy W. *The Village Indians of the Upper Missouri: The Mandans, Hidatsas, and Arikaras.* Lincoln: University of Nebraska Press, 1977.
Robert, Henry Flood, Jr., ed. *The Art of Exploration: The Maximilian-Bodmer Expedition, 1832–34.* A Catalogue to the Expedition; introduction by Miriam Roberts. Omaha: Joslyn Art Museum, 1980.

Acknowledgments

This book would not have been possible without the generous assistance of the Joslyn Art Museum and its Center for Western Studies. I am grateful to Audrey Kauders, Deputy Director; David C. Hunt, Curator for Western American Art; Carol Wyrick, Assistant Curator of Education; Liala Ralph, Museum Shop Manager; Paul Schach, Curator of Manuscripts; and Peggy Henderson, Administrative Assistant.

My thanks also to Louis N. Hafermehl, Director of Archeology and Historic Preservation, North Dakota Heritage Center; and to Fred Armstrong and Tina Whitehorn, National Park Service, Knife River Indian Villages National Historic Site.

Illustrations from the Maximilian-Bodmer Collection are reproduced with permission of the Joslyn Art Museum, Omaha, Nebraska.

Index

(Italicized numbers indicate pages with photos)